COOKIE AURA

Bert Glick

Cover photo: Barbara Feldthouse
Special thanks to Randy Fingland & the Brain Trust

Distributed by Bookpeople
         2929 Fifth Street
         Berkeley, CA 94710
         (415) 549-3030

©copyright 1987 Bert Glick & Crosscut Saw

Second Printing, August 1987

Crosscut Saw
2300-A Roosevelt
Berkeley, CA 94703
(415) 843-7869

ISBN 0-931020-07-7

She said
   I had a cookie aura
      about me
I was sweet
    yet
a crumb at heart
   I for my part
accused her
     of
having a chocolate chip
   on her shoulder
and so
   we nibbled away
at each other
   'til
I melted in her
          mouth

. . . FROM LINDA

Linda my lover stole into my room
    and left
persimmons, pomegranates, & mangoes
        strewn on the pillows
"poets must feed on exotic fruit
    and on flowers too."
        not a trace of a flower in view
within the hour—
        magic violets unviolate my door
Next morning
    without warning
        a PHANTOM sneak attack of love—
bananas, cucumbers, & a hunk of salami
    with another note
        "you are what you eat
        yummmmmmmmmm"

S.O.S.
    Linda the poet stole into my room
        and left
a honeycomb and a swirled green glass bottle
    with a note
        attached to a cork   so designed
        when you remove the cork
    the note pops up
"Help! / am stranded on an island
& / no ship bearing your name
has come in recently / and
I am afraid to swim / to where you
are / all alone / but have drowned
so many times before / what's a risk?
have reason to believe the water may be warm /
or may even part to let (one) of us thru /
these things sometimes happen
        P.S. Please advise on this
matter — whenever / soon
        I miss you."

WHY WE FOUGHT WORLD WAR II

We fought to make the world safe for
   peaceful Japanese/economic/penetration
   Instead of Hiroshima
     We might as well
     have destroyed Detroit
   Or nicknamed the team
     The Toyota Tigers or
     The MoTown Mitsubishis
   Post War World Series:
     IZUZU — 3
     FORD — 1

We fought to make the world safe for
   Volkswagon of America Today—
   Tomorrow the world

We fought to make the world safe for
   Radio Free Europe to pierce
   The Icon Curtain

We fought to make the world safe for
   J.A.P.s
   (Jewish American Princesses)

We fought to make men free
   from the Halls of Silicon Valley
   to the Shores of Mi-am-i

We killed to kill the killing
   so the killers could make a killing
   peacefully

THE PAINTER

To an old prolific Master
Who poked through the haze
          —Claude Monet—

Your poplars
    haystacks of the harvest
    and lillies of the pond
                  forever
Your flowered garden paths
    (planting the irises you painted)
    Japanese draw-bridges
    and misty river bends
Color the soul purple

Reflect sun-ends of our days
    on your shimmering canvas
Pigmentator of well-being
Color therapist

Paint your subliminal cathedrals
    of the heart
Brush away butcheries of the Great War
    with your sublime art
In your concentrated studios
    of countrified peace
The prisms of peace
    dance off your fingertips
Bequeathing to the earth
    the fruits of your palette

ABOUT TIME

Time kills
Greatest known cause of death
Graveyards of schedules to keep
Yet a greater death is to kill time

Old born again friends
Ripe and Rot
In time they are
In time they're not

If time is money
Is energy greed?

Nature invented time
To keep everything from happening at once
Or not at all
(Says graffiti on the wall)

Time equals gravity
(I'm told when you're old)
Breathing down your backbone
Bearing up fine (so far)
In the spine of time

What did Big Ben
Say to the Leaning Tower of Pisa:
"I've got the time
If you've got the inclination"

Better to throw a clock
And see time fly
Than punch (in) a clock
For work despised
Clock watcher

Born in the nick of time
Died in the nick of same

Thank you for your time

GIVE ME THEM OLD TIME FUNDAMENTALIST BLUES!

You can kiss Darwin good-bye
'cause folks don't cotton to his monkey shines
Hauling his evolutionary ass
To court again
For illuminating their schools

You can kiss Anne Frank good-bye
For dying young enough
to still cherish all faiths
of good will
Krishna & Buddha too
So they're axing her too
from school

You can kiss the old German Poet
Good-bye
for saying
All living creatures are cousins

You can kiss Walt Whitman good-bye
for liking the animals because
They don't worship one of their own
Who lived thousands of years ago

You can kiss the Prince of Peace good-bye
For being a pacifist-internationalist

You can kiss Einstein good-bye
For being an internationalist-pacifist

You can kiss Socrates good-bye
For being a polytheistic pagan

You can kiss the White Witch
of the North good-bye
For benign but unGodly magic
and "sayonara"
To the midnight hags of Macbeth
For "Double, double, toil and trouble . . . "

And least of all you can kiss me good-bye
For penning this fart in a whirlwind
Let it be said when I'm dead
I fought Facism half-assedly

MIXED MEDIA MIND MUNCHING MYTH MACHINE

Mistle-toe and TOW Missiles
Heat-seeking kisses
and Adulterous Bible massages that titillate the Lord
and Forbidden Fruit free trading of cocaine futures—
Scandal Fever hits Washington, Wall Street,
and the Electronic Bible Belt of Evangelical Empires—

Booze
    Boobs
        Baubles
            Bibles
                Bribes
                    Blackmail
                        Barbituates
                            Bombs
                                Bonds

And Hostile Takeovers initiated by Satan
all rolled into one
The Unified Scandal Conspiracy to Defraud

And yet
Pity poor Covert War junkies
Passporting drugs
to reinforce their weapons' habit

Today's Civics question:
Is it patriotic to snort Contra coke?

Freedom Snorters:
Get your CIA Freedom Snorter T-Shirt, fellow sinners

"Better than a KGB sex trap."—Saith the Preacher

"Don't think it's been easy
not believing in anything."—I answered

A man's got to believe in something
And I believe
I'll have another scandal

FIRST TUESDAY OF NOVEMBER — TOP OF THE NEWS
"ERECTION EXTRA!" — Toots the headline
I mean "ELECTION EXTRA!"

All the donkeys and elephants
   got me confused
Those well-hung party symbols
   of profane politics
And obscenely expensive exhibitionism
   of private party organs
Discharging civic functions
   record low voter come out

What this country needs
   besides phallic ballots
And candidates handsome as Rock Hudson
   is Prop 69 —
The initiative to ban voting without rubbers
   to insure Safe Politics

MANUAL LABOR OF LOVE

Fits like a glove—
Hand condoms—
Auto eroticize without infecting your hands
Play with your play thing
Without risk
Safe Self Sex
There are no more
'What if' jokes
Because 'what if'
Now is

The future of America is in your hands
Because someone fucked a monkey in Africa

I was told
at a raw encounter group
I was a creep
   who hung-out in subways
         exposing
      himself to women
        another shaft:
    A woman says
    an aging hippie
        is unappealing
After sleeping on it
     I wished I had
         exposed myself

WHAT?

I used to be me
 — I mean
I'm used to being me
 — I mean
I'm used to being used
 — I mean
I used to be used
 — I mean
I used to be used to you
 — I mean
I used to be mean
 — I mean
Amused to be me
 — I mean
If you know what I mean

THE RESUME

        I am
            an accomplished nonachiever
a master of false starts
a practitioner of interesting failures
an artless weaver of awkward first impressions
        I am
            an acknowledged shirker of responsibility
      a professional malingerer-loiterer
a loquacious loafer-harried hairy hanger outer
a wheedling opportunist
a lazy self indulgent gold bricker—Big City Slicker
a seasoned hedonist
a sanctimonious procrastinator

        I am
            a rational voluptuary
an engaging grinner
a reputed carnivore ('With a side of *Bernaise,* please')
   a self made educated bum
   a pro at con
a committed believer in the workings of my universe
a dedicated upholder of my right to play the fool
   Don't call me—
   I'll call you
         (Collect)

"LADIES AND..."

Ladies and Genitalmen:

      I've always been a genitalman
open and above (as they say) board   genital but firm
Always attempt to be a genitalman
      If not
          a genitalman's genitalman
In fact
     I'm a congenital genitalman
Sincerely perspire to be
      a genitalman & a scholar—no sweat
         TRUST me
I promise I'll be genital with you
As the vernal rains fall genitally on thirsty Earth
Like a genital breeze of summer

and my oh so genital touch

      A genital reminder:
A genitalman never comes first—
         holds drawers open

Look into my genital eyes
I've got 2 of them—expanding/contracting&moistening

Genitalmen of the jury
Corpus of my peers
Surely we can reach a genitalman's agreement—Trust me

15?

VAMPIRE WITH WINGS

My roommate
  The Mosquito
    waits late
      for me to bed
        buzzes my head
          believes we are wed—
            My blood the nectar
        of the gods
      she drinks deep
    I can't sleep
No protection
  from her injection
    I Swell from
      her affection
        not to mention
          her bad breath
            & she won't even
          split the rent

ORANGES AND WAR

That victoriously nonviolent
more effective weapon
than an A-Bomb

love-eyed groin-clothed
Mahatma Gandhi

broke his famous fasts
that captured a sub continent

with oranges
and the nectar of prayers
from all faiths of the earth

While

Blimpish Winston Churchill
not wishing to preside
over the dissolution
of the Angloid Empire

always avoided
the frail Indian Liberator
like leprosy

while breakfasting
steaks & ashtrays

SEEING RED

The energy draining anger
Of petty battles
ages us—
Eats away at us

But we bristle
Victimized
By self righteous injustice
Imposed Indignation
      Anger:
Something some people can't live without
      Self Anger:
Often the easiest to unload
More often the hardest
      The opposite of anger:
Forgiveness.

Tension induced rage
Lethal as radiation

The flip side of fury:
Rage as an energizer—
    "I don't get angry
    I get even."—
(Letters emblazed across
a strutting
tee shirt)

That incestuous duo . . .

    Anger & Ego

Wounded egos of the World
    Unite!

Divided
    We fume.

HURT

Hurt is to be
to be savored
to be tossed playfully around
    the cranial cavity
to be weighed-in
    stretching new thresholds
to be coaxed, humored, and dissolved
    into guiltlessness
to be made into metaphor
to mortify and honor
the Hurt

THE NEW HIGH GROUND

They call it
"The new high ground"
Outer (if you will) space
To outflank our earthly enemies honorably
From
Heaven
Above

        Space Wars
         Starring
   The American Archangels
          vs.
   The Soviet Sky Spies

Introducing
Guilt-free lasers
The moral satellite erasers
And other high-tech replacers
of sling shots and
Arrows
From Greeks versus Trojans
To celestial explosions

Onward Christian Computers

EXCATHEDRA

        Hundreds of revolutions
. . . of the earth later

            The Church exonerates Galileo
            Who exonerates the Church?
                  God?

Headline:
Pope absolves Solar System
For its unearthly centeredness

Admits
The mariner of the mind
Discoverer
of moons of Jupiter
Phases of Venus
Meteor marked
Craters of the moon
& skating rink
Rings of Saturn
Suffered
    "From departments of the Church"
            (i.e. Inquisition,
            Celestial oceans
            in a drop of blood)

—Assigns specialists
To study "the Galileo episode"
    (a 350 yr. P.R. beating
        His Holiness hopes to reverse)
Roll over Copernicus
    Tell Newton the news

TALE OF TWO CITIES

    Santa Cruz—
By compelled estimate
10,000 magnitudes sexier than
    Chicago.

More erotic emanations
Per cubic pubic centimeteor in 'Cruz
Than one concrete-gray
Maroon-bricked
Bleak-block
    in Chi-Town

Not a question of
Longitude & latitude as attitude
And profusions of pulchritude
Everywhere you turn
Is to yearn
On every cornier you're hornier
From the morning queue
For the French bakery
(The best buns around)
To any night time boogie down

Senses incessantly assaulted
Battalions of beauties
Armies of the Admired
Delicious deployment
(If little employment)
Torrid battle zone of the sexes

Battered dumb am I

PRURIENT INTEREST

Indian Summer
Pacific Avenue
Duly licensed
Pre-publicized and
Police-escorted
Topless parade
Prurient interest
in feminist nipples
Protruding proudly
Wafted by the warm wind
Politically correct erect
Peep show for a cause
Proclaiming
Women's right
to aire their bosoms
and tan like a man

"But are they good for business?"
Wondered a merchant aloud

"I'm a buttocks person,"
Volunteered a liberated fetishist
from the curb-lined crowd
While TV cameras (boob tube)
Bump and Grind
Hype of the hour
In these days
of Dykes on bykes
and straights on skaights

RIVER VOYEUR

She lives near the river mouth
Her moods changing with the tides
while window-watching from her
gull's eye view of the levee
Herons, shifty sandpipers
Platoons of mud hens
landing in unison
Oscar Levant, the stork, show-off
strutting with
struggling perch
Seals and their sonar coughs to Heaven
Spoonbills
Two-legged joggers
Fishermen salivating for salmon
Emergency pissers
Car-flagging hookers
by the adjacent intersection
Dope deals and rendezvous
Rolling car and strolling fashion shows
Bikers and hikers
overburdened beyond endurance
wrestling with their self-esteem
Strollers infused
with the salt air joy of creation
but next day mope along
following their own funeral
And the daily couple
in their 80's
ambulating arm in arm
like lovers
pair-bonded
like ducks

Putting her own problems on hold
She beholds
from the sliding window
pecking orders of
seagulls
        pigeons
                  and ducks
Vying
for tourists' bread
and fishermen's bait

There
Mountains dip in the distance
Fog seeps in from the valley
She watches three days' worth of weather
In one
The sky rolling with the
Bay driven river

"The Left Bank of the West Coast,
because you're here."

She says, inviting me to share the
Next electrical storm

CURFEWED PARK

Spate of murders
    from the dark

    Sunset-Sunrise
    Someone dies

Pushed in the bush
    grabbed stabbed in the grass
Hoisted & hurled
    off river valley foot-bridge
    Headlong
Dope deal shoot-out
    near the moon-struck pond
And pie-eyed homicide
    by the kiddie slide

    Post-twilight
    Post-mortem
    Zone

Please police
    Deliver us
    from our daily fears
And forgive us
    our nocturnal trespasses
    of the curfewed park
As we forget
    to forgive

Ghost-greenery
    dooming dew
Nightly park lockout
    Don't let crime sleep—
    Muggers
    Thuggers
    Druggers
    Coppers
Get back on the streets
    where you belong
The shrubs
    snooze best
left alone

THREADS OF TIME

Underscoring
    the happening avenue
    of the motley godless
Decked & detached
    in a 30's gown
    eyes dark browned
Crowned by art deco hat
    netting attached
To veil the past
    and noon's June glare
She ambles down the 80's
    on four-inch platinum purple spikes
Nonchalantly electric
    in her early 30's
The pulse of womanhood & fashion
    in search of finesse
And nostalgia
    and the flavor of once upon a time
Come the 90's
    she'll strut the town
In a brocaded gown
    of the 18th century
Buttoned, hooked, and laced
    below Apocalypse in space

OH, BERKELEY

French roll a troll

Out my rent-controlled door
    none of my neighbors conspire with fire
And the Man uniformly ignores (sometimes)
    local and transient Bush People
And bag ladies wheeling carts
    to crash in the park
A metered square block
    off the Milky Way Boulevard of Headlights
Out my window
    where hordes of homeless roam
Home, home in the dark
    in abandoned buildings
    that ignite in the night
Burn alive after five
    Be it ever so humble

Fireplace in a trash can
    Tent City encampment
Boasting "Welcome to Reaganville"
    and "Squatters Go Home"
Winters up in the metered square block
    December dark park
Off the Milky Way Boulevard of Broken Headlights
    out my rent-controlled window

Days and nights in a row
    till the Man blows No
Tearing down Tent Town
    ten minutes point zero
A new world's record·

ALL SHE WONDERS

Pharmaceutically prohibitive
    lamb like paranoia
People awfully audible outside
    she shudders
What's happening around her
    is all she wonders
And everything she does
    she says she feels is wrong
And all she says she knows
    is what she says she needs —
To give love
    to the love needy
It should be so easy
    Instead she takes medicine

TO THE MAN WHO SHARES MY BEAT

On a sun-filled day
    he scopes my eyes
  & drops a word to the wise:
"All this time I haven't busted you
for peddling poems on the Avenue.
Now I want you to write a poem
                about me."
The Squeeze Is On
              I pay poetic protection
              for poetic justice
More & More
      I find
        Officer Walsh's mind
     Quick as a speeding bullet
    his wit tickles me
"You should be a stand-up comedian."
           I say
"You should catch my nightclub act."
              He replies.
              patting the stick
              at his side
We are both writers
   in the same language
     I pen verses
        he tickets
          rhymes & fines
     One lady's poem
       is another lady's
          warrant

CAPTIVE AUDIENCE

Yes,
I still don't have
the nerve
to steal
into a crowded bar
on a Budweiser
Super Bowl
Sunday
Shut off the TV
and in a high-pitched voice
Announce
an impromptu reading
of my latest
unpublished poetry

MIXED NUTS

"This goes to the mixed couple outside."—
said counter lady to co-worker.

"You mean racially mixed couple
or ethnically mixed couple?"

"I mean male-female couple."

"Oh, I didn't think of that."

"Well, these days
you have to think of that."

"What about 'opposite couple'?"

"Okay, this goes to the opposite,
racially homogenous couple outside."

"You mean racially homogenized couple?"

"No, opposite occidental couple."

"You mean racially opposite Caucasian couple
or racially accidental opposite couple?"

"Am I a mixed single?"—
interjected a lone customer.

ETHNIC POEM
or BETTER HE SHOULD MARRY A TREE

In the old days
   it was "He married a *schicksa*!"
Then it was "He married a *Schwarze*!"
   Now it's "He married a *Man*!"
Cyclic progressions of shame
   finely tuned to changing social mores
Molotov! I mean *Mazaltov*!

"My son married a Man!"
   "Is he Jewish?"

THE FALLOPIAN WAY

Loving mother's milk &
    there's a sucker born every minute—
An accomplished metabolist
    of blood, food, & air
Baby Maestro conducting himself
Precocious Lion-Tamer of internal chemistries
    In an eyelash of nativity
Little genius dissolver of complex compounds
    sucking his first breath
    gumming his first meal
    & what a prodigy of elimination
Electronic engineer beyond his year(s)
    pre-natal architect of advanced functional design
Adorably enhanced speck of protoplasm
    Glorified amoeba
From the pond of the womb

THE CRYPTOGRAM

I am
An unabridged
60,000 volume
Code
of time—released
Ciphers
Crystallized in seconds
Curved
Contour & symmetry
a symphony of systems
of gaseous creation
& stellar Composition
Fathomed from
mists of moisture
a nerve storm of excitement
a hot bed of
        Motion & motive
        Membrane & memory
        Tissue & tears
a steaming stew
of its own juices
a mortal mystery
with a hundred billion butlers—
(All of whom did it)
a breathing breeding
Brooding being
Out of a blue
    (Stellar mist)

THE PLANETS

When the Sun was young and strong
    star shadows stretched long
Pluto basked and teemed
    singing its solar song
(Pre-Industrial Neptune steamed
    Mars a hovering oven of red meat
Saturn a half-baked floating dream-
    murmur of the future)
The Plutonic year generations
    It took to say 'Good Day.'
Metabolic sedations and forever to expire
    Ocean of slow motion
The maturing rays receded
    life-kissing every planet with its memories
Nearer the solar root
    Spring in outer space
From solar systems to nervous systems
    We're 3rd from the bottom rung
    High strung rapid fire
Hazy hothouse Venus waiting in the wings
    to inherit the worn torn crown of consciousness
Zanier than ever
    her cloud shroud breaking cobalt blue
Beneath the dwindling vigor
    of the wine-colored Sun
Mercury—
    Last chance for a fast shuffle

FILET OF SOLAR

Time and space
Scramble
Like ham and eggs
On a flying saucer
—Hold the greasy galaxy—
Catsup with the hash burnt quasars
and a pinch of spicy
Black hole sauce
Where no flavor can escape
Jelly
    The constant comet
                    Cosmos and
Butter
    The eonic muffins
We order in orbit
While the cook
    Flips
The heavens
From day to night
    (Meteor rare)
on his stardust spatula
and what's the universe
Without coffee—
The speed of life
Check, please,
        I'm
            falling

LIKE

    Like
Capillaries and veins
    Stretching
    to the sky
The leafless limbs
of the giant oak
    Dominate
The downtown parking lot
    Defiantly
Rooted in remembrance
& already cracked asphalt
Atmospherelessly black
    Its overgrown
    Nerve ganglia
    Framed by sky
Sometimes sustains me
    Amidst
The muck of day
When I walk by
Energy uprush of the Earth
    Parking lot tree
of good & evil knowledge

FOAMY BOULDERS

Unshrouded in mystery
    Unfog bound
The looming boulders
    Unfolding
Off the shores
    of southern Oregon
I visually devoured

Clustered choirs of rock
    congregate
        in
        the
        water
        &
    Psalm the beach
Lost land
    once joined to the edge
Now possessed & lapped
        by the sea
Stupendous Face Rock
Chiselled
By day & dark
Silhouettes
The clear-etched face
Of an Indian Princess
Of legend and lore
And swirling battles
With backs to the sea
'Round red stained sands
The last stands
Off the contested continent

FLOWERFUL

Wind-tossed
Near the river
Naked ladies bloom
Up coast
and in forests and valleys
Hot earth readies
for their trumpet-shaped shades
of ruby-toned
Beauty

The highlight of
Twilight
Teasing the
    sun's glare
Summer's insignias
Proud beauties
From the bush
In
   ooh's
      and
         ah's

they grow
in mortal peril
Their shimmering
Allure
So pluckable

VERNAL INVOICE

Step into my wood-paneled office
    by the side of the creek
the atmosphere — relaxed here
    Kick off your shoes and soak your feet
The Earth baked rocks — my Danish-modern
    for our lounging comfort

My secretary the squirrel, eternally out to lunch
    can't stand dictation
Luckily, I'm a lenient boss

The plants around here
              are working overtime
      business is so good
  I have several branch offices
              sprouting up stream
Finally Spring
      and I'm branching out
       Time and a half

NIGHT AND DAY

Dear
Trick of nature *deja vu:*
As you know
The scent of the cooling creek
On warm nights
Plucks chords of pre-natal mystic memory

    Gropingly
Writing in the woods
Near some kind of berry bush
While minuscule crazy critters
Land on my steno pad
Crawling between summer-stagnated
Words and meter
    Suddenly
I saw
a tiny darting dinosaur
(Lizard-sized realization
Of pre-historic shrinkage
To accommodate
My pea-sized brain)

    Glacially yours,
        Bert

THE WOOD CHOPPER

Somehow   I felt unnative
    semitic   desperate
An object of suspicion
    almost deviant
Compared to the upright
    square-jawed rugged out-of-doors
Cigarette billboard ad-like ax-wielding
    wood chopper
Encountered in the autumn-inflamed
    red-yellow-gold-green-brown-orange
Leaved woods
    of mountain creek Oregon park
This morning

"Hello" — he said
    unjudging and upbeat   between whacks

"Hi" — I replied judgingly
    schlepping in beauty

Prism colored carpet
    of myriad fallen leaves
Cushions heavy footfalls
    of anxiety
Ceaseless groping against gravity
    and addictions
Alias life

MOZART NEVER SLEPT HERE

They don't want you out Taking an old fashioned walk
In exit strewn L.A.
                Ay—
                        Ay—

No hills in Chicago
No ambulators in L.A.
No sidewalks in Beverly Hills
Guided tours are okay
                kay—
                        Kay—

Want to walk?
Stroll on your grounds

Don't have any?
You're out of bounds

Mansion on the mountain
Desolate splendor
Empty opulence
Gilded isolation
Old movie mogul playpen with
A 360 degree view of
The 70 degree haze &
Smudged night lights of the Valley
Where you pay—
              pay—
In L.A.
      Mozart is compelled to disco
                          go—
                              go—

Land of media central
And the home
Of home entertainment
Market researched
Life

This is only a test
                Test—

WINTER WEST

Rain and Recession

         'Depression' says Hoover
         'Panic' says Taft
         'Crisis' say
         Classic analysts of economic hardball:
         'Crisis of '93'

'Imaginary crisis—
Don't panic—
Avoid depression—
Just recede like a hairline
                Quietly—'
blips the orbiting satellite
    of economic indicators

Loudly
The rain taxes the valley
Garnishing the hills for mud slides
& downpours of deficits downtown
but air like wine between cloudbursts
in the town of wave-lashed wharves of shattered glass
Recession of the shore line

Seven year dollar drought
Followed by flash floods of doubt—
blips the debt-compounding satellite
of orbiting stagflation

TROUBLED LOVE

"You hump from the heart."
                She said
and that disturbs her
                knowing
He'll hurt from the heart
                When she leaves
        * * *

Too many pretty resentments
Too many minor
Unaddressed grievances
                Salted
By too many secret tears
an accumulation
of too many hurts
Herded in her heart
                Triggering
an absence of too many years
        * * *

I heard you crying in the shower
Louder than the pelting water

I must have blamed it on relationships

a good cry
is a sweet release

Then you dripped dry
by the window

She's loathe to trade
a possessive husband
for jealous lovers:

"These clingers & clutchers"
She refrains—
"If only they knew
unjealously excites me
Freedom draws us closer
and independence
whets my hunger."

* *

Wives
Who come to me
Complain
The flip side of passion
Is possession and pain
Chains of joy or
Fear of freedom
The slow poison
of self sacrifice
and unlove
(the suppressed stuff of cancer)
or
The children's shattered security
of Mom's terrible swift exit

Issues
We chop & chew
Till we're blue

* *

* *

After the cyclone quarrel
that shred their
       home
              in pieces
She bolts
    and roams the streets
under her cloud   wrung dry
      weatherbeaten & approached
by night-time stray wolves
She hobbles home
       finding
the chessboard
ready on the bed
all pieces in place
except the king and queen
facing off
      stageboard center
framed by rose petals
exquisite peace offering
Mate-mending her heart   again

PSSST!

Open heart secrecy
No secret the secrets behind your eyes
         All kinds—

    —professional   secrets
    —state   secrets
    —top secret   secrets
    —sex   secrets
    —bathroom   secrets
    —body   secrets
    —office   secrets
    —relationship   secrets
    —anxiety   secrets
    —narcotic   secrets
    —closet & cupboard   secrets
    —breach of confidence   secrets
    —die of embarrassment adolescent   secrets
    —Historic   secrets

Lethal secrets like a Venus Fly Trap
Behind every promise lies a secret
The secrets we keep
& the ones we share
Some we secrete
Some we don't care
Some we cocoon from jelly womb
to marble tomb

We all have the same secrets
        Some forgotten

SAY WHEN

When compassion is the fashion
When losers save face with effacing grace
      & winners are fashionably late
When money is mute & double talk cute
When margin for error increases geometrically
When mystery loses its novelty
When comfort & encouragement are found around
                          every corner &
                climaxes   ordered on
                          command
When gravity is pinned to the mat & cries 'Uncle'
When 'out of harms way' means not stepping
                        on sidewalk cracks
When those who are wise declare salvation
                        lies in belly button
                        fuzz
When for comic relief we laugh at the grief &
                        for birthday gifts—
                        the sky
                  I'll be there
              (if I feel like it)

MIRRORING

        Once
I applied for a job
        in a new abandoned building
Then ran a football
        thru a poppy field of sleep-walkers
I'm partially awake
        I'm told
(Sometimes snoring
        between parenthesis)
        Once
I kissed your eyelids
        while you were sleeping
Redeeming me in your
        subterranean eye
        Twice
When we waken Let's
        boogie to the nearest haunt
'neath the 'We reserve
        the right
        To refuse service
        To the nervous'
Sign overhead—
        There I'll succumb
        to your succulent symbols
        of compassion
        Thrice . . .
        in the age of you
Glad to be born
If they ask what I
        remember most—
        Your infectious laughter
When you look into
        the heart of the abyss
It peers into
        the heart of you
        Mirroring.

A SHOULDER TO CRAYON

Sophia *enfant terrible*
Eats crayons by the fistful
Her magenta most likely livered
Her kidneys silvered
A green spleen like Halloween
Proud purple heart
Her rainbow digestion
Prismatic intestine
Hues of the spectrum   dapple her diaper
The ruby speckled
                         — yellow spangled
                             orange tinted
                             lung
for the young
& so forth & chromatic so on
By the dye of the crayon

What eons to chew on under three

HONOR THY FATHER

As a growing girl, she was
    chastised at dinner
by, of all people, her father
    (chinaware everywhere)
for not washing, of all things,
    her hands
"Go upstairs, Sarah,
    and scrub them—
        immediately,"
he would say—
    repeatedly
day after day.

                      Behind the bathroom door
                          she would meticulously
                              NOT wash her hands
                      Unsudsed digitals

Daddy never suspected
    as he inspected
    her germ-laden little fingers,
"That's much better,"
  he said—
    with satisfaction
    forgetting his hemorrhoids

FUMBLE FINGERED ETERNITY

        Aging—
Uprighteous grappling with gravity
Eliminating trivia along the way—
Memory more select
Time mostly meters his face—
        Crow's feet—laugh lines
        and tear eroded gullies
He walks younger naked
Hands wrinkled warmly
        Chin sprouts
        white hairs
here and there—
        pluck, pluck

Poor bearded baby
A Senior post-adolescent
        prematurely young
It's ethical to be flexible—
        pluck, pluck

        Accelerating time
        Everyone over 40 knows
        the older you are
the faster it goes

        All he did as a kid
        had the aura of eons
Taking fumble-fingered eternity
to tie his shoes

IN DAYS OF WOE
DAD WENT TO WOO

Deflated—
        Related—
                      Depression days
When tomatoes were cheaper
                      & sweethearts a dime
                      dearer
She was the niece of a bum-a-round buddy
of Dad's.
        They met & melted in the Bronx
        of hard knocks
        His wild heart heisted
We find he pined
            from the snowy vacuum
            of Chicago
& wired a ring & a ticket
Destination:
La Salle St. Station
She detrained at Grandma's
(Mother's mother-in-law-to-be)
            Proper
in her own separate
Wallpapered quarters
(But Dad walked in his sleep)

THE OCTOGENARIAN

Approaching my father's 80th birthday
   makes me feel young for my age
      I've retired
      he still works
I think he's a shyster lawyer
He thinks I'm a paper poet
Shyster lawyers & paper poets bleed in the tweed
   so we
         understand
         one-in-other
What to send him for a birthday present?
            a hard-on?
Better to keep it for myself
I'm sure he'd say
         (Sept. '74)

         (a year has passed)
My eighty year old octopappy
(knowing he's mortal
         dyes his grey hair dark brown
not because he's vain
It's better for business he claims)
is coming to town
         but first
he has to close a real estate deal
No wonder
      he calls me
           a communist gypsy
In the same vein
a judge in court
     accused me
of watching the world
         go by
I held my tongue
I wasn't his son

MOTHER'S DAY

After all
         these years
  my Mother of Sorrows
          finally
  had a   good dream
          about me
          she said
          instead of
  her usual nightmares

In place of
         my stricken body
  face down in a
  gutter splattered
  pool of blood
         somewhere
   on the West Coast
Instead of
   nodding in some
         cobwebbed drool
         with AIDS
   & other dissipated
          related
         diseases

She dreamt
  I came a-knockin'
         at her door
         all spruced up
         smelling of Old Spice
         decked out in a
         3 pieced
         white shirted—silk tied—Summer suit
  saying
         "Hi! Thought
         I'd surprise you."

(A letter from my 84 yr. old unretired father)

      Law Offices   ROOM 1600
ALEXANDER H. GLICK   134 N. La Salle Street
                                      Chicago, Ill. 60602

Phone: CEntral 6-3110

                                      October, 1978

Dear Bert—

    Never get over-excited or lose your temper. Many deaths etc. result from that = Just two days ago, a neighbor's nephew was killed by another boy over a small traffic accident!

        <u>Keep Your Cool!</u>

    Don't over lift = never aid a motorist in pushing a car etc. = It is dangerous for the heart & causes hernia etc. Play it safe & smart! These little suggestions will lead to a long life = & enjoyable one.

    Eat the simple & proper foods! <u>No salts</u> — very little if necessary. Plenty fresh water. Feet clean & change of socks. Spend money on socks & <u>two pairs of shoes</u> = That is a must.

    Why don't you go in for <u>novels</u> & <u>fiction</u>!?? or go in for <u>poetry</u> etc. with rhythm etc. & more substantial subjects = no profanity.

        <u>Call Sunday with out fail.</u>

                                          Love Dad

Insignia of Endurance
My papa's ancient neck

Creased-creviced
Flu proof testimony to the ages

        Not even his almost boyish
hands of 87
or unbandied legs
whisking him still with ease
where they unhampered please

or his dyed dark brown hair
can beyond compare
        to his stately, ancient neck
and irrepressible Adam's Apple mirth
("My only pains are in the pocket book")

Cosmetic burden
shock absorbing buffer
of shriveling time
        for his bentless frame

        Majestic isthmus—
        (Bearer of the Panama hat)

                Nov. '81

SEPTEMBER MOURN

September mourn for a dead dad
Pavane for mama's mate
of 50 years plus one

Time to cremate
Golden anniversary after glow
as warm breezes blow
off the Great Lake

(Abraham buried Sarah
and shed a tear or two, they say)

88 years under the sun
Being old before I was born
He was wise when I was young
A far better father than I a son

Half mischievous—pain erasing
Mona Lisa Death smile
that seems to say
'I pulled a fast one on you this time'

Euphoria of Oblivion

DELIVERANCE

In days when 'relate'
   was a meaningless case
and I loaded a welfare worker
   In cold broken Chicago
They sent me to 90 yr Anna
   from the Old Country
Take the El to Hell
   then knock-knock a spell
Door inches open
               the breadth of a chain
Shriveled pile of wrinkles
   peers thru eyes of muted pain
Eking out the words
   in her tragic accent:
               "Are you come to kill me?"
As if I were an Angel of death
   in corduroys

"No. I'm from the County."

BUS BELLE

    From
The flush-cheeked
Red-sweatered
Olympian heights
of her adolescent bloom
She buses your table
    Blushingly
Wiping your mess
Gathering your garbage
Her dapper apron flapping

Under the skylight
She stands
Mustard-stained hands on her hips
    Poised
Ready to spring
To scrub & clean
Making work fun (for a season)
Somehow maternal and all knowing
Sweet dame fifteen

A SILVER BLUR

A silver blur
Greyhound bound

pretzel twisted
oldish man

cane and small
suitcase in hand

hurrying
hobbling

on the crippled double
to the local depot

thru the swirling
California

Youth Beauty
Extravaganza
downtown

Unseen
except by the
Aging Fearful

FOR VITO — ON HIS 74TH BIRTHDAY (ON GOING)

Injustice rubs him raw
So he goes dancing in costume
As a dirt-besmirched tramp (seasoned punk)
Or immaculate Spanish padre
In black cape, cap, and cross
My favorite septogenarian friend
Has tenure on the dance floor
Women attuned to his seniority
To his somersaulting madcap capering
In movement to the music
Able to walk the length of a log on his hands
In his robust age
Clown white prancing protestor
Still procreates and rears litters of kids—
Combination Cassanova and Pa Kettle
I'm sure he'll bang on 30 birthdays more
The trek of people to his door
Some bearing chunks of oak and redwood
To be carved with a flair
Master sculptor chisels time

Update:
Vito and his girlfriend
Win 2nd place in an operatic
Lip synch contest
Then French kiss out the door.

THE CURTAIN RAZOR

The day Stalin
>>sold the Polacks
>>down the river
>>(the Rhine, that is)
>>to buy time, he'd say

I was born
>>Daylight
>>Terror
>>Savings

in Chicago
>>(Where 'Cash register' is
>>a 'Jewish piano')

>>on the cusp
of Leo-Virgo
Soviet-Nazi
>>Non-Aggression Pact
>>signed & sealed in
>>Moscow

Molotov & von Ribbentrop
>>unvexed by plausible deniability
>>& other effluvia
>>of cover-your-derriere-
>>Democracy

Clinking cocktails
>>toasting the birth
>>of World War II

>>and me

ANGEL DUST

His mind
Venturing
Beyond where
The eye sees

His big-boned
Brutal hands
Carve
Angels
Out of gnarly oaks
Wood nymphs from walnut
and witches out of hemlock

The master sculptor
Of the Santa Cruz Mountains
Magician of the woods
Displaced downtown
Hotel bound
He varnishes and sands
With his gnarly hands
In the noon gloom of his room
Underselling his treasures
But not his heart

PAMELA POEMS

Rewarding me for merely being
she has hot bath water running
when I awaken
              the only words she spoke:
              "Go soak."
Affecting affectionate fun
she dubs me in the tub
Sir Gorgeous Hunk
I was tempted to believe her

Morning Promenade

Strolling the sunny-side-up
what a cute couple
              our shadows make
    obeying that impulse
    she gooses me
    middle of the intersection
    like a true Christian
    I turned the other cheek

Poem from Pamela on the Road:

He offered me his park boudoir
and made me his Queen for a Day
or two.
        During my reign
I lovingly possessed
              caressed
                  &
              undressed
his family jewels   so
as you search the California sunset
for the perfect shadow couple   remember
Daylight Savings Time
                is just a state of
                mind
On the misty verge of May

                    "God
                    Bless
                    You
            On your birthday"
                    The
                    Book
                    Mark
                    Said
Gold emblazoned letters
                    on a field of Satin red
            Pinned   to the door
of my favorite Aquarian Athiest
                            For her birthday
She never guessed
                I was the Holy Ghost
I knocked religiously
Her sun-refracted
                Stained glassed smile
"I promise we'll make love."—
        Said she—
"If first we meditate."

"I don't have the patience of a Saint."—
        I sighed.
"You're with a Saint."
        She replied.

LAPIDARY

Your hypnotic
    Snake-like
        Knotted necklace
            of fine cut
          Crystals
           that cling
          to your bosom
          and gleam
     as you move
     & heave
Little burgundy
    Kiss sparks
       of liquid light
            Shiny leaping
            Yesses
            from the fireworks
            of your breasts
        and crystalline dance
            of your eyes

TABOO

Fragrances of
    our intimacies
        captured
    in my facial
           foliage
Long After
        our
        loving acts

        in course
        of day
           numerous whiffs
    spontaneous replay
I shall not shave
        to save my soul

Balding in heaven
        Bearded in hell

Whorizontal Hooker

with a digital watch

(a real looker)

Wraps her lithe arms

around

The down-thrusting neck

Upgazing wrist — watcher

announcing

"Time's up, honey!"

Digital interruptus

I REMEMBER BABY DOLL

The big black mama
        who deflowered
        & devoured me
        twenty years ago
    on the south side of Chicago
for 5 U.S. dollars
        died yesterday
        I read in the
        San Francisco Chronicle
        (her picture included)
in an anonymous profession
        her death covered
        coast-to-coast
the number of her lovers
        must be legion
        ranging from freaks
        in Cotati to judges
        on the Supreme Court
the Mid-night special
        leaving for the big
        Bordello in the sky
Baby Doll rides again

                July, '74

THE GOOD HOUSEKEEPING SEAL OF APPROVAL
or
"DAD, CAN I HAVE ANOTHER PIPEFUL?"

"Are the dishes done, dear?" —
    asks the loving father
Doling out drugs   to his doting daughter
    for all chores performed —
No wonder the house is spotless

Another public service blurb
    not brought to you
        by the President's Commission on Drug Abuse
Craving martial law enforcement
    and mandatory urine analysis
Monitored and thermometered
    for freshness sake
At all places of worship
    to weed out wee-wees with weed wherever

So when bayonet soldiers
    bearing empty bottles
For the loving father's daughter
    to fill
With her golden drops
    at the ice cream parlor
Where she scoops part-time
    We may or may not hear,
"Fuck you and the dishes, dad!"

STOCKS AND BONDAGE

The Dow Jones fluctuates
the average variations
the Bulls vs the Bears
the Russian Bears?
or the Chicago Bears?
or the Nuclear Bears?

Does Dow tell Jones?
does Marx tell Engels?
or does Engels tell Jones?
on the QT? Or over the counter?
Or at half time?

The Czars of Wall St.
Those prestigious firms
since the 19th century
Dow & Jones
and Marx & Engels
merge
in a series of interlocking multi-national
inside trading hostile takeovers
of the People's Commissariat
to concoct an ideological Frankenstein
with sickles, balls, and stripes
forever

"You're just sour grapes."—said
a Computer Block Trader

SATURDAY AFTERNOON HYMN

The dyed-in-the-dacron
               suit wearing
               Bible bearing
               drum thumping
               gospel warbling
               pamphlet pressing
                    Christians
    proselytize
                    the Avenue
                    of the Damned
    recognize
      with sure and
           unctuous instinct
               Satan Hymnself
           treating me with
           utmost respect & civility

Perfunctorily polite bows
                      they let me pass by
     you can't
         convert
      The Prince of Darkness
        Best not to try

TRUTH IN ADVERTISING

Struck by
    Top of the morn
    Soft core kiddie porn
Newspaper centerfold
    Towering ten year old
In tights & leotards
    That don't retard
Suspiciously well-developed
    Possibly touched-up
Market researched
    Legs
Standing spread-eagled
    Her eye level crotch
(Or-am-I-imagining-it?)
    Thrust in our faces
For adult dollars
    Her budding outfit
A la Emporium Capwell
    Back-to-school Sex Sell

We decent minded citizens
    Should be aroused at this

HEADLONG HEADLINE

"Jump, jump!"

Shouts
The tired-of-waiting
Thrill-hungry-crowd
To the would-be suicider
     Wavering
On the 14th floor ledge
Urging him
To dent the cement
& consummate a memory of a lifetime
Climax the day with death
Hope for a headlong leap

Then go home and gossip
Before sleep

JINGLE BELLS

By the nub of the flurry
December's violinists of the Avenue
Serenade you
Serene tunes
Celebrating
The Prince of Peace
for kindly donations
No strings attached
Silver Bells . . .
While I sip
Gourmet caffeine
from Insurgent Guatamala
Hells Bells . . .
And those perennial Solstice Troopers—
The Salvation Army
Should be seen
Jangling their bells
in downtown Beirut
Ringing out the Marines
Christmas time in the city
Sip, sip
Jingle, jingle

CHARCOAL OF A RICH REVOLUTIONARY

He's a rich revolutionary
        a doctrinaire
        Marxist millionaire
        A real estate magnate who
Echoes
        'Property is theft'
Left & Right

Exploit or be exploited
in exploitive society
He explains
Without anxiety

He loves to lend
to capitalists
He hates
at high rates
and Collect their collateral
Upon default
Practicing
Private philanthropy
on the side
World wide

He calls me
a gentleman
Because
I never ask for money
When we meet

DINNER AT THE RITZ

                                           Beat the system!
                             The gourmet Garbage Man
               Can
          Doesn't spend a dime
   Scarfing
A la
    Pacific Garden Mall garbage
               Cans
                      (cylindrical smorgasbords)
                      open air banquet hall

              Sometimes still warm nutritious chow
        Doesn't care who sees him anyhow
   Your trash = his dessert
Half consumed cuisine
   Bon Apetit!
       Can't beat
            3 squares a day
               Bloated midnight snacker
               Matted hair & blanket in
       Hand
     The Garbage man
       Can
              Rent—food & lint free
              The scavenger of the Avenue
       Meets the Bourgeoisie
   Or maybe
 He's a millionaire in drag
like a 30's movie

Bon Apetit!

"THIN WITHIN"

"My compassion for FAT people
    a degree more distant
        than for children."
          —She demured.
            Slouched upon her couch

"What about aging THIN neurotics with beards
    Who hunger to be younger
        Who gorge, but don't gain
            Substituting one appetite for another."
          —he dead-panned
        Across the sputtering wick

"I'd prefer young suicidals
      with French accents
           Although Anorexia is a hard act to swallow
        so, I don't begrudge
           Your bearded gorger."
        —She grinned
        guzzling a Diet something

Another strand
        in the tangled yarn
        of old/young
        slender/plump
          Illusions
            or
Is a fat masochist
a glutton for punishment?

THRU FRESH BLOSSOMED BREEZES

He can't feed the birds
  Coffee
    Cigarettes or
      Drugs
And doesn't toss croissants
  to
    trespassing
      puppies
In the Old World Replica
  cobblestoned
    fabricated plaza
      Central Coast Style
For genteel Computer Nerds
  exchanging invitations
    to mandatory
      slide shows
But does drool
  over neo-
    Szechuan
      noodles
At oodles
  of bodies beautiful queueing
    for the California
      Try-It Diet Bar
In this Peeping Time
  of apparent peace
    thru fresh blossomed
      breezes

LONDON FOG

In
   a London coffee shop
     a long time ago
     I asked a young
            woman
        from
           The Continent
       if   she was single
          She replied in
          a thick accent
      "I'm double."
I
  nervously
      laughed
  and left
  not being equal
to the situation

YANKEE DOODLE

"What do you think
    of 45 degree angles?"
      I asked her
doodling in quiet despair
      "I Love 'em.
          If it weren't
      for 45 degree angles
        We wouldn't be here."
        She answered.
      "Do you like them better
    than 90 degree angles?"
    I pursued.
  She thought a second
         "Yes"
  Then someone nearby
     caught her eye
  at a 45 degree angle
She
  departed my table

AN EMBARRASSING SITUATION

Lounging in a dark restaurant bar
    a couple of friends & I
  & half-a-slice-of-apple-pie
      left by a peachy lady
      at a table nearby
        (which was wishful thinking)

She hadn't left the premises—
      she went to the bathroom
      returning momentarily
        only to see me
        wolfing her pie

"I don't want to talk about it,
      but how *could* you"
        was the look
        in her eye

Moral:
In crust we trust

18TH CENTURY GOURMET GOSSIP COLUMN

While Voltaire lost his teeth
gorging rich Diets of Napoleons,
Bismarcks & Kaiser rolls
at the court of Frederick the Great
poor Rousseau
suffered uremia penuriously

On the lighter side:
Those aristocrats of cuisine
The Earl of Sandwich
and the Duc de Mayonnaise
spread it on thick
hamming it up for reporters
over their Caesar salads and
Salisbury steaks.
Sounds like a case for Dr. Graham Cracker

King of the sugar addicts:
Louis XVI
his 600 pastry cooks,
just a custard memory,
meets Dr. Guillotine,
Capping off our
Let-them-eat-cake-century.

Gotta deep freeze now
catch you in a year hundred or two,
Exchanging my goose quill for a MacIntosh
Grinding out more *rat-a-tat-tat*
just as juxtapositionally
thru the miraculous musical mucous
of living gluttony
as the beacon of hypocrisy
shines thru the mists of history.

SHE

She gave him peacock feathers
from her closet of discarded plumage

> "Should I put them in water
> so they don't wilt?" — he asked
> "or discolor?"

> "No. Honor them at room temperature."
> — She replied.

   * * *

Waiting 20 years for him
on a nonchalant corner
in her clairvoyant colors
> She stayed young
> so he'd recognize her

DEDICATED TO MRS. P.

The dread in our head
Ten times worse than reality
All there is to fear
Is fear itself—we've said

To be un-hospital-bound a blessing
To view healthy people on T.V.
From a sick-ridden bed
Or watch them come and go
From a shut-in's window

To pass from death brushing pain
To comfort and ease
What infinite relief

To be up and out
Is what life's about

The ambulatory pleasures
Of buying a scarf
Or breathing fresh after-rain's air
Along the barefoot beach

The undisability of sweet mobility
Of all freedoms the profoundest is health—
      Enjoy

HANDLE WITH INTENSIVE CARE

Dream-domed
Germ-doomed   purging surgery
    Drainage of the ages
       Entangling tubes   of despair   everywhere
Excuse my abscessed absence
While I contemplate my bile
    flowing through the tube
    in my nose   like the Nile
And oh
the lip-smacking   intra-venous grub
    glucose a la carte
    tubular cafeteria
And the catheter   in me   too intimate
I'm near hysteria
    But don't worry folks,
    I'll be soft shoein'it again soon
No sweat
No temperature

NURSEHOOD

Not the world's oldest
    But it's most needed
                    profession
From maidenhood to womanhood to nursehood
    Sainthood wedded to sensuality
                  Secular nuns
The husbands and lovers
    in their lives
For the earthly appetites
                  Nurse Service—
Singularly human and uncasual
    From placentas to deadman's bedpans
They tend

I was the patient of Saints
    Who saw
               my weaknesses, frailties and strengths
    I saw
               their having-seen-it-all patience
They know most secrets

ACE IN THE HOLISTIC

Let us play Holistic poker

Your blood-shot iridology
betrays your bluff
internal espionage

I'll see your chakra
and raise you 2 one-eyed yogis

Your double deuce aura
won't do.
My herbal flush takes
the jacuzzi.

Jack of Hearts
needs martial arts
Pair of eights
meditates
I'm a non smoker joker
wild card

7 Chakra Draw

A game for gambling gurus
and well heeled healer dealers
Shut up and heal

Vegetarian table steaks with sprouts
Organic ante

'While you're up,
would you bring the keefir and reefer, please?
This hand is a pain in the neck
at this juncture

I need some acupuncture'

My ace in the Holistic

DANCE OR DIE

She's the ballerina
    of the will to heal
Choreographer   of the wheelchair prone
    pirouetting upper torsos
Dance therapist
    of the disabled
Concert mistress
    of syncopated paralytics
Soft shoe hoofer
    of the hobbling afflicted
Choral maestro
    of the unresigned confined
Jazzercising rejuvenator
    of the recovering talented
Prima donna of dedication
    life-pulse-rhythm-reviver
Brushing breath
    into the heart of the stroke

SOME UNFATHOMED METAPHOR

A Ballast of the Brain
Gives Birth Through My Mouth
    or
How I Coughed Up A Pearl
(A True Story)

Once I produced from the roof of my mouth
   a slowly growing gorgeously ovalesque
Alabaster white saliva-coated
Palate Stone
   the size of a golf ball
Hitting the Delivery Room floor
   with a thud and a bounce
Making, I was told, medical history
   in Petaluma — The Egg Capital of the World

However, I still won't try to start
   a new religion

To trace
Sources of inner selfishness
Scarcity inspired stinginess
Forever misremember
It pays to be generous
Undigested lesson
Unswallowed whole
To treat a friend like a stranger
Short-sighted relapse
Into ancient states of mind
From warm-hearted banter
to silent animosity
to mortally offend
a valued friend who
takes 'no' like a dagger

MAINSTREAM MONGER

To better promote myself
I'll get
My own personal business card

Which interested parties
Could pick their teeth with
After taking me to lunch

All kidding aside
What this card would say
Is premature if not immaterial
Followed by weighty credentials:

And in this corner
a Perennial Groper
In the Darkness of (Un)deserved Obscurity
And Co-con-founder
Of the American Academy and Institute
of Instability
Facile advice
Instant Intuition
Cheap

WHEELS OF REVOLUTION

Who invented the wheel? — he wondered —
Cruising Van Ness
In Lisa's clunker Buick
Beyond
      Glass-domed Mercedes displays
On the road to half way house Truth
Hiding in our domed skulls:
No one can reserve
Hurtling Earth
Except to die and park
(Boxed or metered)
        So crept his question:

   "What would change after a revolution?"

   "That Murphy Cadillac sign" —
She pointed
"Would reappear
Karl Marx Cadillac."
That night
they dreamt
of revolution on Car Row:

        Marx Mercury
        Mao Motors
        Che' Chevrolet
        Uncle Ho's Hondas
        Lenin's Lincolns —
        (Loans and lease)

Must have been something they ate
At Stalin's Steak House

NO MINORS PROGRAMMED

Garden Mall Old West bar
   buffalo heads and cowboy stars
old rifles and new antiques
   brass fixtures oak and teak
      meet
the automated liquor-is-quicker computer
   button pusher digital bartender
programmed release like a robot lover
   pharmaceutically pure
      40 spouts for 40 drinks
piped to the Big Bottles in the Vault
   burping forth their fifths —
remote control — precise portions
   unbiased ounces — no drip to the drops
Codified schnaaps
   electronic fizz
   no free shots for free loaders
The great leveler computer
   monitors & liquidates
      bar fly favorites
      water chasers
      and Happy Hour Patriots.

and no tips for the buttons
   Mostly I remember
   the empty bottles for show
   like magnum mannikins in a window

NO ONE'S FAULT
BUT
5.9 ON THE RICHTER

Mother Earth
          most powerful poet
                            .
                        . .

When She speaks . . . . you are moved
                           . .
                         .
            TERRA   FIRMA   *SQUIRMA*
         O
MORNING J L T before first bite
      Fork to omlette . . .
                              A
                 omlette   W
                             A
                              Y

  ll
 o i   e
R n   v through the floor
   g   a
  w w
   a e
    v

   Clatter   of   matter
L E A P from chair and HUG the wall
   embracing her
            Clima
             x

WICKED WEATHER

Slightly deadly
        drizzle
Polluted pennies
        from Heaven
on our way
to the Mind Police Cafe

"Acid rain!"—
        she cried
as the drops
not mascara
stung her eyes

Darting under the freeway
        for cover
She recovers
        her color

"Why didn't it sting my eyes?"—
        I ask her
"Because you're already desensitized."—
        She replies.

Transcontinental
    ground grown food
             poisoning
    and Statue of Liberty
    and other shrine
    corroding
    Cancer of the clouds

Even
Rain Forest
Deodorant Spray
may not help someday
on our way
to the
Mind Police Cafe

ZIG ZAG

Jesus & I
were both busted
   in occupied Jerusalem
at supposedly   different points
                          in time
        for supposedly different
                      crimes
in the very land he encountered
                       Mary Magdalene
          and said:
          "Let he who is without sin cast the
          stone," I got stoned
and then met my wife Susan
                     a dark eyed Hashemite beauty
from Brooklyn
            in a shady Arab cafe
              Boy meets girl
    we made love & peed in the bushes
              on Mt. Zion
    overlooking hallowed halls
                  of ancient worship
Now, chapters later.   I see her
                  occasionally
           in occupied
                Berkeley

JERUSALEM JAIL

Curve ceilinged
Arabesque architecture
Over arching
Cigarette butt bishops and
Gum wrapper rooks
Improvised chess —
In the old Jerusalem jail
and enough hashish
Smuggled in
to smooth   edges of captivity
In the land of Nativity
The Israeli underworld
    My cell mates
    a few
    like a dark sparkle-eyed
    Moroccan Jew
    Politely propositioning me
    I
    Younger and fairer
    Than now
    Politely declining
    Thanks anyhow
    Relations in the hoosegow
    Confining
    and delicate

You meet some of the gentlest people in
                                jail
                              psycho wards
                              and riots

VANITY OF VANITIES PRESS

    Vanity of Vanities Press
      — or —
    Ego a-go go I'm from Chicago
      — or —
    Tickled to be Poet of the Gross National Product
        Good 'ole GNP
      — or —
    How many trees felled to print these pages
        metaphoric deforestration
        all for vanity and toothpicks
      — or —
What a main stream perspirator am I
    Riding the current
      — or —
    Song of the Saw
These pages sing to me
I am a redwood
I am a willow
Pine poem lovely as a tree
      — or —
We've been through the mill together

HAPPY HOUR(S)

"Isn't there anything   more fundamental
You do with time   besides bare poetry?"—
     She babbled   perched on a bar stool
        loose legs   dangling shapely

"Something weighty   like stacking bricks?"—
     I shot back   thru stale   Hell's Waiting Room
     layers of smoke

"Guilty Hour!
Beers dime a glass   for the guilty!"—
     foamed the bartender   already swamped

"Did I strike   a sore spot   with you?"—
     She pursued   pouring a pitcher-full

Suppressing rage   I disengage
Then showing 'em what for   cartwheel out the door

       *   *   *

An old school chum   now heading
The head hunting:
        I-Owe-I-Owe-Off-to-Work-I-Go
        Mundane-Monday-Money-Employment-Agency
Reports
No orders for poets in the hopper
Kind of sad — He said   distant-eyed
Although   a more attractive prospective non-employer kibbitzer
     mockingly complains
My poetry isn't crazed enough   not enough rage

       *   *   *

And yet   another buddy
Put it to me
     The world doesn't need   my minor poetry
I was compelled to agree
So I ate my words   and then swallowed my pen
Eliminating   commas & periods   out the other end

TIDBITS

Everything in moderation including moderation

* *

The Writers' National Anthem:
Oh Say
Can You Say
What You See

* *

Chimpanzees smoke like chimneys
A pacifying monkey puffs a Lucky
Other mammels light camels
As a zoological joke
(only after meals
and making love)

* *

Is   death
the   way
it   is
    before
we're born?

    Answers
vary
amongst the living

* *

When sick
The first step
Is to dream you've healed